ELLA'S BRIGHT LIGHT SERIES
BOOK ONE

God's First Creations

HARRIETT LYNN SMITH
A.K.A. - GRAND MOMMA

ISBN: 9798873627615
Imprint: Independently published

Ella's Bright Light

BOOK 1 – *God's First Creations*

HARRIETT LYNN SMITH

A.K.A. – *Grand Momma*

Dedication

To my delightful Granddaughter, Ella Sofia, her parents, Laura Elizabeth and Samuli, and her Auntie Jayne Marie – know that my love for each of you will abide FOREVER!

Grand Momma

"Lord, in the beginning you made the earth.
And your hands made the skies."
Hebrews 1:10 (ICB)

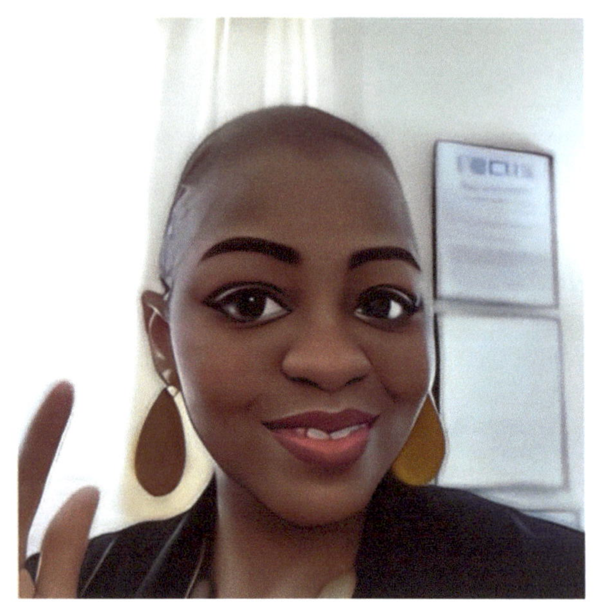

My Darling Ella,

*My prayer is simple. I pray that you would clearly **hear** God's Word, **understand** God's Word, **believe** God's Word, and **receive** God's Word that you might fully **obey** God's Word. Simply put, I ask for nothing more and nothing less than God's Word to take root and produce fruit in your life every day that you might be full of great joy! In Jesus' Name I pray. Amen.*

- Grand Momma

Have you ever been afraid of the dark?

ME, TOO.

But you know what?

In Genesis Chapter 1, **GOD SAID**...

"Let there be... light!" And light began to shine.

God saw the light, and he knew that it was good.

Then... he **separated** the light from the darkness.

God named the light

"DAY,"

and

He named the darkness

"NIGHT."

Ahh ...

There was evening, and then there was morning.

This was the

1ˢᵗ DAY.

(Genesis 1:3-5)

BELOVED, LET'S PRAY

Lord, thank you for the light.
Now I can see that I don't
have to be afraid of the dark.
Amen.

Have you ever been on an airplane and flew over beautiful waters?

Can you guess what God made on the 2nd Day?

NO... *God did not make an airplane.*

He made something much **MORE IMPORTANT!**

You see, after He made light,

then **GOD SAID** …

"Let there be a space!"

And do you know what God called that space?

God named the space ... "SKY."

Wow! Do you know what that means?

Now we can buy our own tickets!
Board the big plane and fly!

I can visit my Grand Momma
		and my Auntie Jayne!

I can visit my G-Pa and my G-Ma!

And,
I can go visit all my cousins, too!

Ahh ...

There was evening, and then there was morning.

This was the

(Genesis 1:6-8)

BELOVED, LET'S PRAY

Lord, thank you for making the sky.

Now we can go visit each other.

We'll simply board a plane and fly.

Amen.

After the first day when God made light,

so that you and I could see...

And after the second day when God made the sky,

Knowing we'd buy plane tickets one day, and fly.

Then came the third day.

And Genesis chapter 1 goes on to say,

GOD SAID... **"Let the water under the sky be gathered together so that the dry land will appear."**

And God saw that this was good.

Then **GOD SAID** …

"Let the earth grow **grass**, **plants** and **fruit trees**."

And it happened …
Just like God said.

The earth grew grass
and plants.

And it grew trees that made
fruit with seeds in it.

Every plant made its own kind of seeds.
And God saw that this was good.

Ahh ...

There was evening, and then there was morning.

This was the

(Genesis 1:9-13)

BELOVED, LET'S PRAY

Lord, thank you for making the earth and having it grow beautiful grass, wonderful plants, and all kinds of delicious fruit trees.

Amen.

Ella, you have a birthday coming up, don't you?

How old will you be on your next birthday?

How Old?

Oh, my goodness!

And that's a special occasion, isn't it?

Did you know that God thinks you're pretty special, too?

Let's continue this story from Genesis chapter 1, and you'll see what I mean.

Then **GOD SAID** ...

"Let there be lights in the sky."

These lights will separate the days from the nights.

"They will be used for **signs to show when special meetings begin** *and* **to show the days and years."**

*"They will be in the sky
to shine light on the earth."*

And it happened ...
Just like God said.

He made the larger light to rule during the day.

He made the smaller light to rule during the night.

Do you know what God called the larger light that we see in the sky?

And what did God call the smaller light we see in the sky at night?

Oh... and God also made the *twinkle, twinkle little* stars.

And God saw that this was good.

Ahh ...

There was evening, and then there was morning.

This was the

(Genesis 1:14-19)

BELOVED, LET'S PRAY

Lord, thank you for making the sun, the moon, and the stars! Now we know when to celebrate special days... like **my birthday** on April 5th and **your birthday** at Christmas time.

Amen.

Have you ever been to an Aquarium?

What do you
know about
sea life?

Then you also need to know that on the fifth day,
GOD SAID …

"Let the water be filled with many living things…"

"And let there be birds to fly in the air over the earth."

And
It happened...
Just like God
said.

So, **God created** large sea animals,
And all the many living things in the sea.

God also created every kind of bird that flies in the air.

And God saw that this was good.

But this time when God saw that it was good ...

He smiled on them.

And He told them to do something very special.

Now, what do you suppose God told them to do?

The FISH and the BIRDS did what God told them to do.

Ahh ...

There was evening, and then there was morning.

This was the

5th DAY.

(Genesis 1:20-23)

BELOVED, LET'S PRAY

Lord, thank you for making all the large and small fish that swim in the water. And thank you for making all the beautiful birds that fly in the air.

Amen.

Have you ever been to the zoo?

What kind of animals did you see at the zoo?

What is your favorite animal?

If you like animals, then you will really like what God created on the 6th day!

In Genesis chapter 1, **GOD SAID** ...

"Let the earth produce many kinds of living things. Let there be many different kinds of animals."

"Let there be LARGE animals."

"... and SMALL crawling animals of every kind."

"And let all these animals produce more animals."

... Just like God said.

So, God made every kind of animal.

And God saw that this was good.

Then **GOD SAID** ...

"Now let's make people who will be like us."

*"They will rule over all the large animals
and all the little things that crawl on the earth."*

And unlike _any_ of the animals,
God created people in his own image.
That means God created people to be like himself.

God smiled on them and **SAID TO THEM**...
"Have many children.
Fill the earth and take control of it."

Wow! God looked at everything he had made...

And he saw that everything was **VERY GOOD.**

Ahh ...

There was evening, and then there was morning.

This was the

6ᵗʰ DAY.

(Genesis 1:24-31)

BELOVED, LET'S PRAY

Lord, You made EVERYTHING!
And everything belongs to YOU.

Thank you for making my family,
and all of my friends, too.

And Lord, thank you for making me!

Amen.

What do you do at the end of your day?

You rest, don't you?
Me, too!

We usually rest because we're tired, don't we?

But did you know that on the 7th day, God rested?

Yes, God rested…

But not because He was tired.

God saw that everything He made was **VERY GOOD.**

God rested because HE WAS FINISHED
with His work of creation.

"God blessed the seventh day and made it a holy day."

That means ...

"He made it special."

Why? "Because on that day God rested
from all the work he did while creating the world."

(Genesis 2:1-3)

Remember your Creator while you are young.

Ecclesiastes 12:1 ICB

The earth and everything on it belong to the LORD.

The world and all its people belong to him.

Psalm 24:1 ERV

Know that the Lord,

He *is* God;

It is He *who* has made us,

and not we ourselves;

Psalm 100:3 NKJV

BELOVED, LET'S PRAY

"Lord, I look at the heavens you made with your hands. I see the moon and the stars you created."

(Psalm 8:3)

You even made me!
And Lord, I won't forget.

Thank you for being <u>my</u> Creator!

Amen.

My darling, Granddaughter,

THIS IS THE FIRST OF GOD'S CREATIONS!

Happy 5th Birthday, Ella Sofia!

With Love from Grand Momma

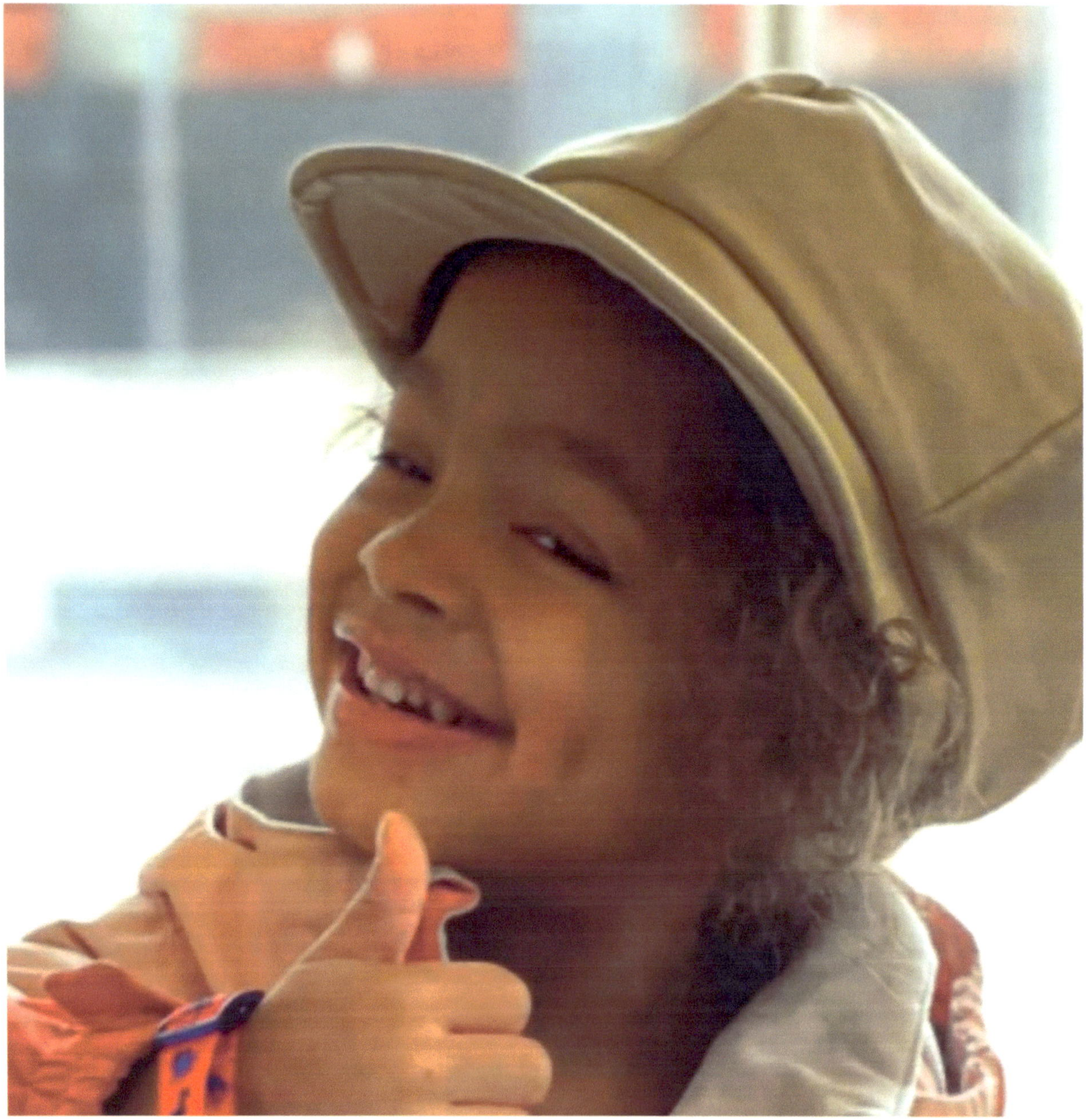

Ella's Bright Light

"God's First Creations"

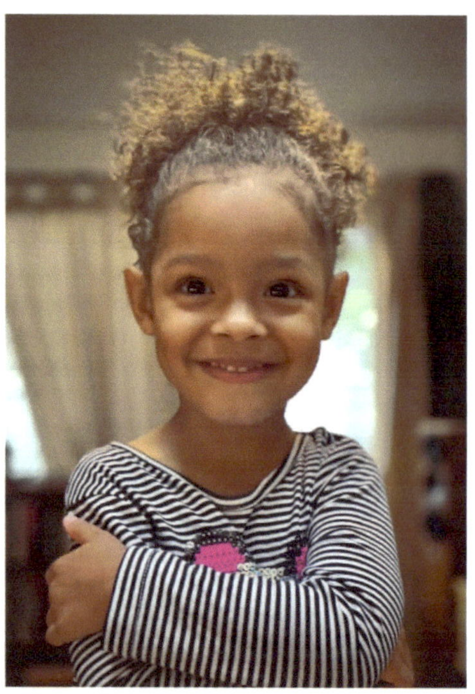

Ella Sofia

THE END

Until Next Time

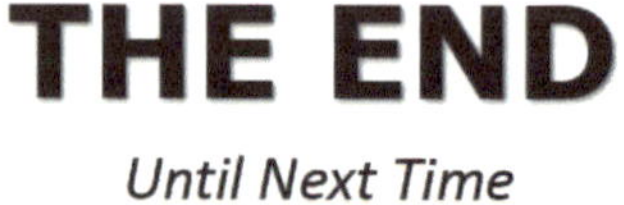

About the Author

HARRIETT LYNN SMITH is the Founder **Pure Prominence Media**, an audio production company creating inspirational media for today's secular markets.

As an inspirational writer, creative producer, and biblically sound teacher, Harriett has worked with many churches and parachurch ministries as led by the Spirit of God throughout the United States for over 40 years.

Today, she writes and produces various audiograms, devotionals, books, and training manuals to equip the Body of Christ as she teaches interactive webinars on effective evangelism and genuine Christian discipleship.

Residing in North Carolina, Harriett enjoys the rich Word and simplicity of Vision RDU under the pastoral leadership of Jerome Gay, Jr. where the focus is to Glorify God and Make Disciples - for this is truly her life-long mission.

9 798330 241712